The Indian Ocean

by Anne Ylvisaker

W9-ATZ-396

Consultant:
Sarah E. Schoedinger
Education Coordinator
Consortium for Oceanographic Research and Education
Washington, D.C.

Bridgestone Books
an imprint of Capstone Press
Mankato, Minnesota

Bridgestone Books are published by Capstone Press
151 Good Counsel Drive, P.O. Box 669, Mankato, Minnesota 56002
http://www.capstonepress.com

Library of Congress Cataloging-in-Publication Data
Ylvisaker, Anne.
The Indian Ocean / by Anne Ylvisaker.
    p. cm.—(Oceans)
    Includes bibliographical references and index.
    Summary: Introduces the ocean that lies between Australia and Asia, and provides
instructions for an activity to demonstrate how to remove the salt from salt water.
    ISBN 0-7368-3420-6 (softcover) ISBN 0-7368-1425-6 (hardcover)
    1. Oceanography—Indian Ocean—Juvenile literature. [1. Indian Ocean.
2. Oceanography.] I. Title.
GC721 .Y58 2003
551.46'7—dc21   2001007909

Editorial Credits

Megan Schoeneberger, editor; Karen Risch, product planning editor; Linda Clavel,
    designer; Image Select International, photo researcher

Photo Credits

Art Directors and TRIP/Dinodia, 14; Art Directors and TRIP/S. Tierney, 8 (photo);
Corbis/Arne Hodalic, 16; Corbis/Steve Kaufman, 12; Digital Vision, cover; Digital
Wisdom/Mountain High, 6, 8 (map); Erin Scott/SARIN Creative, 10; Jack Deutsch/Stock
South/PictureQuest, 18; Katz Pictures/Jim Lukoski, 20; PhotoDisc, Inc., 4; RubberBall
Productions, 22, 23

Table of Contents

The Indian Ocean 5

The Location of the Indian Ocean 7

The Depth of the Indian Ocean 9

The Bottom of the Indian Ocean 11

The Water in the Indian Ocean 13

The Climate around the Indian Ocean 15

Animals in the Indian Ocean 17

Plants in the Indian Ocean 19

Keeping the Indian Ocean Healthy 21

Hands On: Getting the Salt out of Salt Water 22

Words to Know 23

Read More 23

Internet Sites 24

Index. 24

The Indian Ocean

The Indian Ocean is the third largest ocean. It covers about 26 million square miles (67 million square kilometers). The Indian Ocean is about the size of Africa and Asia put together.

ASIA

PACIFIC
OCEAN

AFRICA

INDONESIA

ATLANTIC
OCEAN

AUSTRALIA

INDIAN OCEAN

N

W ◄◆► E

S

| | Indian Ocean |
| | Other water areas |

ANTARCTIC OCEAN

ANTARCTICA

The Location of the Indian Ocean

The Indian Ocean meets Australia, Indonesia, and the Pacific Ocean on the east. Africa and the Atlantic Ocean border the Indian Ocean to the west. Asia lies to the north. The Antarctic Ocean forms the southern border.

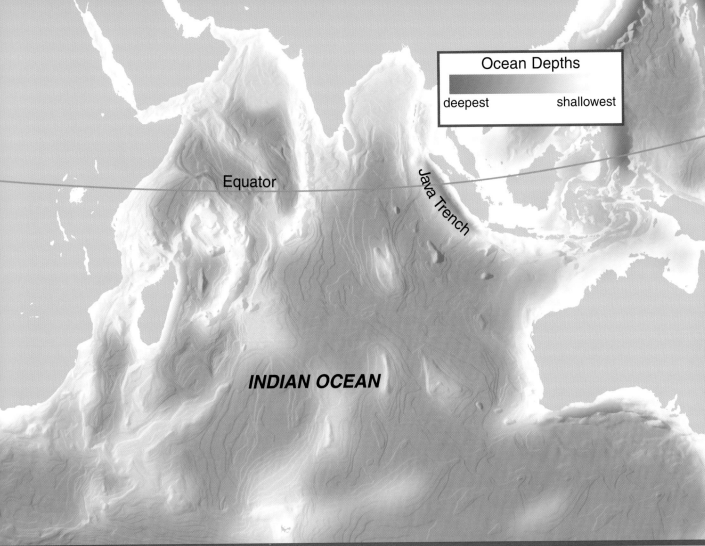

Equator   Java Trench

INDIAN OCEAN

People use scuba gear to dive below the ocean's surface. They can study plants and animals in the ocean. But people can dive only about 190 feet (58 meters). They need underwater vehicles called submersibles (suhb-MUHR-si-buhls) to dive to the deepest parts of the ocean.

8

The Depth of the Indian Ocean

The average depth of the Indian Ocean is 12,785 feet (3,897 meters). That is more than 2 miles (3 kilometers) deep. The deepest place in the Indian Ocean is the Java Trench. There, the Indian Ocean is more than 4 miles (6 kilometers) deep.

depth
a measure of how deep something is

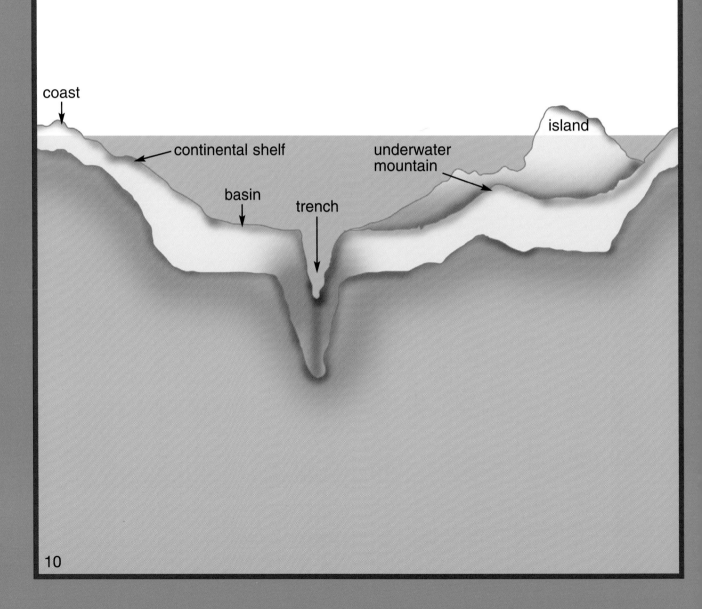

coast

continental shelf

island

underwater mountain

basin

trench

10

The Bottom of the Indian Ocean

The Indian Ocean has a narrow continental shelf. It slopes from the coast to the basin. The basin of the Indian Ocean has hills, trenches, and flat areas. The Mid-Indian Ridge is an underwater mountain range. Volcanoes also rise from the ocean basin.

basin
the low, flat part of an ocean's floor

Fun Fact
The Red Sea, shown here, is the saltiest part of the Indian Ocean.

The Water in the Indian Ocean

The water in the Indian Ocean is salty and warm. Sunlight warms water near the ocean's surface. The temperature of the Indian Ocean's water can reach 85 degrees Fahrenheit (29 degrees Celsius). It is warmest near the equator.

equator
an imaginary line around the middle of Earth

Fun Fact
Monsoon winds change directions with the seasons. Warm winds from the southwest blow from May to September. Cool winds from the northeast blow from November to March.

The Climate around the Indian Ocean

The climate around the Indian Ocean can be windy and rainy. Monsoons blow over the northern Indian Ocean. These strong winds cause large waves and large amounts of rainfall. Storms called typhoons sometimes happen in the Indian Ocean during summer.

climate

the usual weather that occurs in a place

Mudskipper gobies live along the coast of the Indian Ocean. These big-eyed fish can crawl out of the ocean onto land. They use their strong fins to move around. They can even climb mangrove trees near the shore.

Animals in the Indian Ocean

Many animals live in the Indian Ocean.
Blue whales and leatherback sea turtles
swim in the Indian Ocean. The turtles
lay eggs on nearby islands. Fish and
eels hide in coral reefs. Dugongs live
in the warm water of the Indian Ocean.

mangrove tree

a type of tree that grows
along the coasts of many
warm oceans and seas

Plants in the Indian Ocean

Most ocean plants grow in shallow water. Sea grass and other seaweeds grow near coral reefs. Phytoplankton float near the Indian Ocean's surface. These tiny plants are food for many ocean animals. Mangrove trees grow in mud along the coast.

shallow
not deep

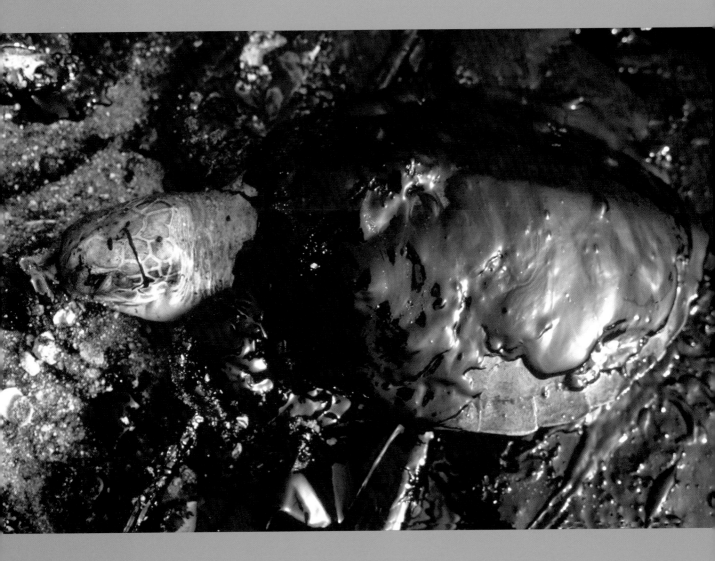

Keeping the Indian Ocean Healthy

Plants and animals need clean water. Oil spills have hurt the Indian Ocean. The world's largest oil spill happened in the Indian Ocean in 1991. Many birds died. Sea turtles, whales, and other animals also died.

Hands On: Getting the Salt out of Salt Water

Ocean water is salty. You can get the salt out of the water.

What You Need

Water
1-cup (250-mL) measuring cup
2 tablespoons (30 mL) table salt
Paintbrush
Sheet of colored construction paper
Hair dryer
Adult helper

What You Do

1. Measure 1 cup (250 mL) of water in the measuring cup.
2. Add the salt to the water. Use your paintbrush to stir it well.
3. Use the brush to cover the paper with salt water.
4. With your adult helper, use the hair dryer to dry the paper. Crystals of salt will be left on the paper.

Water turns into water vapor when it is heated. Water vapor cannot be seen. When you heat the water with the hair dryer, the water turns into a gas. Only the salt stays on the paper.

Words to Know

average (AV-uh-rij)—the most common amount of something; an average amount is found by adding figures together and dividing by the number of figures.

continental shelf (KON-tuh-nuhn-tuhl SHELF)—the shallow area of an ocean's floor near a coast

coral reef (KOR-uhl REEF)—an area of coral skeletons near the surface of the ocean

dugong (DOO-gong)—a large, plant-eating mammal that is related to a manatee; dugongs have a rounded nose, a streamlined body, and a lobed tail like whales.

monsoon (mon-SOON)—a strong, seasonal wind

phytoplankton (FITE-oh-plangk-tuhn)—tiny plants that drift in oceans; phytoplankton are too small to be seen without a microscope.

surface (SUR-fiss)—the top or outside layer of something

trench (TRENCH)—a long, narrow valley in an ocean

typhoon (tye-FOON)—a powerful storm with high winds and large waves; typhoons are very much like the hurricanes that happen in the Atlantic Ocean.

Read More

Prevost, John F. *The Indian Ocean.* Oceans and Seas. Minneapolis: Abdo, 2000.

Taylor, L. R. (Leighton R.) *The Indian Ocean.* Life at the Sea. Woodbridge, Conn.: Blackbirch Press, 1998.

Internet Sites

Oceanlink
http://www.oceanlink.island.net
The Sea
http://www.seasky.org/sea.html

Index

basin, 11
birds, 21
climate, 15
continental shelf, 11
coral reefs, 17, 19
depth, 9
dugongs, 17
equator, 13
fish, 16, 17
Java Trench, 9
mangrove trees, 16, 19
Mid-Indian Ridge, 11
monsoon, 14, 15
mudskipper gobies, 16

oil spill, 21
phytoplankton, 19
plants, 8, 19, 21
rainfall, 15
Red Sea, 12
salt, 12, 13
scuba, 8
sea turtles, 17, 21
size of ocean, 5
temperature, 13
trench, 9, 11
typhoons, 15
whales, 17, 21
wind, 14, 15